QUAKERPSALMS
A Book of Devotions

Compiled and arranged
by T.H.S.Wallace

New Foundation Publications
Camp Hill, PA, USA
2002

Published in the United States of America
by New Foundation Publications.
Printed on acid-free paper.

No part of this publication may be reproduced,
stored in a retrieval system, or transmitted in any
form or by any means, electronic, mechanical, or
otherwise, without the written permission of the
publisher: New Foundation Publications, 3032
Logan Street, Camp Hill, PA 17011.

Library of Congress
Cataloguing-in-Publication Data

QuakerPsalms: A Book of Devotions

p.   cm.

ISBN 0-9701375-1-6
Library of Congress Catalog Card Number:

Acknowledgments: The editors are indebted to
Donna Gentile for her excellent design work and
helpful suggestions during the preparation of the
manuscript for publication.

Cover and book design by Donna Gentile.

Contents

QUAKERPSALMS
from the Journal of George Fox

QUAKERPSALMS:
from the Epistles of George Fox

Epilogue

Preface

This little volume of *QuakerPsalms* has long been a project that I wanted to attempt. The germ of its conception was planted nearly 20 years ago when the late Joseph Pickvance, a British scholar of George Fox's 17th century ministry, sent me a poetic version of the latter's great 267th epistle, "Sing and Rejoice, You Children of the Day and of the Light." The Psalmic qualities of the epistle were immediately evident in Joe's version and a letter accompanying his poetic rendering noted that there were many more epistles and passages in Fox's *Works* that might be similarly treated.

Fox, whose untiring gospel labors led to the founding of the Religious Society of Friends (Quakers), has left us his *Journal*, a momentous spiritual classic of two volumes; several hundred epistles in another two volumes deemed by generations of readers as classics of pastoral advice; four volumes of *Doctrinals*—and extensive unpublished correspondence and other writings. A man of prodigious intellect and profound spiritual experience, Fox had committed almost the whole of Scripture to memory by the age of 21. He swam in and through it, his contemporaries claimed, as naturally as a fish in the sea, but—even more important—he possessed a profound and intimate spiritual knowledge of Scripture that rivals, and sometimes surpasses, our modern understanding of *The Book.*

I had been reading Fox's *Works* for some years before Pickvance's sample came into my hands, and, as an English professor and poet, I recognized the verbal power and poetic qualities of the best of Fox's *Works,* power and qualities he had obviously absorbed from Scripture, that great literary storehouse that has profoundly influenced so much of what is best in British and American literature. Fox had developed an energetic style of proclaiming the gospel. Since his *Works* themselves were largely dictated, they carry the intimate, yet intense, rhythms of his speaking voice, a voice that stirred people throughout England, Europe, and the sparsely settled American colonies, with the call to experience the redemptive power of God and presence of Christ.

The *QuakerPsalms* within this little volume are drawn largely from two sources: Fox's *Journal* and his *Epistles* as presented in the 1831 edition of his *Works,* which were recently reprinted by the New Foundation Publications. Those psalms drawn from Fox's *Journal* are identified by the volume and page from which they are taken. Psalms from the *Epistles* are more simply identified by the numbers of those epistles from which they are drawn.

As an artist, I have taken some liberties with the original texts, rhetorical liberties, poetic liberties, not liberties in substance. Each QuakerPsalm aims at capturing and preserving the essential points of Fox's message. However, to improve readability, I have modernized language in places, reduced the redundancy (which was a natural and important part of 17th century preaching style), smoothed out the occasional awkward phrase, and compressed Fox's language where it was simple to do so. My license is, I trust, only poetic.

Of course, only certain epistles and some passages of the *Journal* lend themselves to poetic transfiguration. Other epistles were teaching instruments, and still others addressed at length problems and pastoral needs of the faithful. However, there remain those that—in times of need, error, confusion, persecution, and suffering—rise in Spirit, language, rhetoric, and inspiration, to high poetry and are well worth experiencing and reading. In each of these, I have carefully sought to capture the rhythm of the original composition/delivery in the lining of the work and sometimes one can still hear the impressive preaching style of the 17th century.

T.H.S.Wallace
Camp Hill, Pennsylvania
September 1, 2002

An Introduction to *QuakerPsalms* and How to Read Them

Like the original biblical *Psalms*, the following *QuakerPsalms* are meant to be manna, food in the wilderness of the world. They have many of the qualities of the great psalms of faith, praise, and exhortation, and a durability akin to their older forebearers. I have worked in the hopes that those who read these pages with the eyes of faith might be encouraged and edified by George Fox's great faith, vision, and understanding of the gospel, encouraged and edified as were his original listeners and readers.

QuakerPsalms: Psalms of Triumphant Faith

Yet, while *QuakerPsalms* are similar to their Old Testament forebearers, they also possess a key difference. Our Old Testament psalms are often wretched cries, from a people who are unconfident, outwardly aware of evil's staggering power and seeming triumph. Their passionate, honest expression of our struggle for faith have endeared them to all generations of Judeo-Christian readers, generations that have found their own condition too aptly expressed of course. There are great moments of triumphant, clear moments in which God's power is experienced, and these are much cherished.

Our *QuakerPsalms* are the psalms of a people who have thoroughly experienced the presence and power of their Lord, who seek to do Christ's will, and who find the power in Him to be obedient. *QuakerPsalms* draw upon the profound Christian revelation of the New Testament and evidence one of the truest understandings of that revelation, one of the most complete expressions of Christian faith since the apostolic age. In short, *QuakerPsalms* contain the poetry of a triumphant Christianity, not the politically triumphant Christianity of Empire and sword, but a Christianity that possesses a faith victorious over temptation, sin, and evil in this world.

QuakerPsalms: Their Challenge to Our Time

QuakerPsalms challenge much of what passes for Christianity in our day. The faith that undergirds *QuakerPsalms* is not the weak faith of Puritan England, which preached up the power of sin and denied God's power and love to save men and women from it in this life. The faith witnessed in these psalms is a faith that looks to Jesus Christ for the power to keep His commandments *and finds that power given!* The faith testified to here is one that has the power to unify Christ's church and overcome all manner of persecution, suffering, and death. These psalms speak of a faith that bears the good fruits of love, meekness, patience, kindness, steadfastness, honesty, and faithfulness—and is identified by those fruits. These psalms testify to a faith that stands for righteousness, opposes deceit, and is utterly resistant to evil, which it fights with spiritual, not physical, weapons. *QuakerPsalms* proclaim a faith that seeks the good of all, for God would have all to be redeemed.

One critical observer of early Friends noted with grudging admiration that Quakers were the most Christian of all Christians, for while others made a profession of believing in Jesus Christ, early Friends found His living presence at the very center of their faith, their lives, their community, and the gospel. Christ for them is far more than the bringer of good news: *He is the good news!* Christ Jesus for them is far more than Christ crucified for our sins: *He is also Christ risen, present, and leading His people.* Christ Jesus is no figurehead of the Church: *He is the living, active head—its priest, shepherd, bishop, counselor, peacemaker, king, prophet, governor, and teacher.* He, in reality, holds all the offices of His church.

How To Read *QuakerPsalms*

To read these psalms rightly, one must step back from traditional Catholic and Protestant doctrine, for what George Fox is saying here goes back to early Christianity and its foundation: the experience of the risen Christ revealing Himself to His people and directing their work in His world. In fact, when we compare the effects of the early Christian revelation with the early Quaker revelation and witness, we see both possessed a living sense of God's power and love—and the lives of faithful people in both groups bear testimony that indeed their faith was radically different from that of the world around them. Their effect on the world around them was to turn it upside down by their utter faithfulness. These *QuakerPsalms* witness to the Truth and they have the credentials to prove it.

QuakerPsalms are best read slowly, carefully, contemplatively. Look for gems of observation and advice, unusual and startling phrasing, which speak of a profound experience and understanding of the work of the Spirit. Look for gems and you'll find them in profusion. For instance, Fox's "QuakerPsalm 15: Sound, Sound Abroad, You Faithful Servants," his rousing call to ministry, when read carefully, yields deep truths concerning what good ministry is. The passage below is just one of many possible examples from its text:

> Sound the pleasant melodious
> sound. Sound, sound you the trumpets,
> the melodious sound aboard,
>
> that all the deaf ears may be opened
> to hear the trumpet's pleasant sound
> to judgment and Life, condemnation
>
> and Light.

Fox is not speaking of hell and brimstone here. He is speaking instead of the work of redemption. Proclaiming the gospel is not a task of terrorizing people into salvation. For Fox, it is a beautiful work, a task of the heart. The message is pleasant, melodious, delightful, a relief to the pained and panting heart that opens to receive it. One doesn't often think of the trumpet's sound to judgment and condemnation as pleasant, until one realizes Fox is describing conversion and the conviction of wrongdoing and wrong living that is part of that experience, not merely the Last Judgment. The judgment and condemning that takes place at conversion and after it, the judgment and condemning of what is wrong within us, is indeed pleasant when we realize that Christ Jesus has the power to bring us out of our bondage to evil. He gives us the power to turn away from what is killing us and to turn to something far better: Life and the

Light of Jesus Christ. Fox gives us a whole vision of the good news: the gospel is not preached to condemn people, but to bring them to a far, far better thing!

At times, Fox takes the imagery of Scripture and opens it in a new and living way. In the same QuakerPsalm as above, after exhorting ministers to call men and women to the living, the resurrected Christ present within, for He's risen from the dead, Fox transforms the traditional image of guards and visitors at Christ's tomb into a surprising metaphor for those who have been waiting and looking for Christ in the wrong place:

> Sound, sound, you trumpets of the Lord—
>
> to all the seekers of the living
> among the dead in the graves that
> the watchers keep—that He's risen,
>
> He's not in the grave. He's risen.
> There's that under the grave of the
> watchers of the outward grave,
>
> which must be awakened and come
> to hear His voice that they might live.

Fox recognizes many people are inwardly dead. Worse, they watch outwardly for Christ Jesus in a place they cannot find Him, thus they are "watchers of the outward grave." They still seek the living Christ among the spiritually dead, even those who guard the tomb against His resurrection! Under all that deadness, "under the grave of watchers," is that of God— that hunger and thirst for God—which must be awakened, so people can hear Christ's voice and know His presence within. The transfiguration of grave-guarding in Gethsemani into a fresh, living, neatly turned, and creative metaphor is as good as poetry gets—and it deserves our careful consideration for the fresh spiritual insights it is meant to convey.

These *QuakerPsalms*, likewise, correct our faulty and disturbing misunderstanding of Christ's gospel. For instance, the media tell us repeatedly, to the point of utter cliché, that the present ecological mess is due to the fact that the patriarchal Judeo-Christian tradition endorses the subduing and domination of every living thing to human exploitation (Gen.1:28). However, Fox sets the record straight, for he tells us that such a view comes from a false and twisted faith typical of humanity in the Fall. In QuakerPsalm 49, which ends this volume, Fox explains that humanity redeemed by the gospel of Christ sees and treats the world differently. Christ leads us to see the earth once more as a paradise, the garden of God. It is only when Christ Jesus cures us of the blindness that has led us to rape the earth that we see how God has ordered it and "how all creatures stand in their places,/ keeping their unity" with all creation. It is not the Judeo-Christian tradition that's at fault: it's our human refusal to hear and obey our Creator and thus live in unity with His creation.

Reading *QuakerPsalms* in the Spirit

Last, but certainly not least, these *QuakerPsalms* are meant to be read with the eyes of faith, eyes opened by Jesus Christ to the Truth behind the words. George Fox, himself, observed that words alone are inadequate to communicate the Truth of God. He notes that the Jews of Jesus' time had the Scriptures, at least in the form of the Old Testament, but the written words in and of themselves were insufficient to bring them to a recognition of the Christ. Fox compared their experience with that of people in his own time (1630s to 1690s) and observed "how people read the Scriptures without a right sense of them, and without duly applying them to their own states" [*Journal* 31]. Thus, his apostolic mission was:

> to turn people from darkness to the light that they might receive Christ Jesus, for to as many as should receive him in his light, I saw that he would give power to become the sons of God, which I had obtained by receiving Christ. And I was to direct people to the Spirit that gave forth the Scriptures, by which they might be led into all Truth, and so up to Christ and God, as they had been who gave them forth [*Journal* 34].

For Fox and the early Quakers, it was the Spirit that opened the Truth within the words of Scripture—and one cannot rightly and fully understand the Scriptures unless they are "opened" or interpreted by Christ. Seeking our living and present Teacher to reveal the true meaning of Scripture brings us to the true source of authority in things spiritual—not *The Book* alone—but Christ Jesus who interprets it.

What is true of reading the Scriptures is true for reading this little book: Seek first what Jesus Christ, The Word of God, reveals to you in these *QuakerPsalms*. Like Scripture, they were composed in the Spirit, written to be read and understood on a deeper level than simply the intellectual. They speak of God's and

Christ's ongoing revelation of themselves to us and open the momentous possibility of bringing our lives into full communion with, and complete obedience to, our Lord, Creator, and Shepherd.

A Note on the Life and Faith of George Fox

Historians today often term George Fox as the founder of the Religious Society of Friends, better known as the Quakers. However, he, himself, would have said that he was commissioned by his Lord to call people again to the pure faith of Christ Jesus, the prophets, and the apostles—the faith of the early Christians. His *Journal* and the two volumes of his *Epistles* are classics of Christian literature.

Coming of age in the North of England in a time of great religious and social upheaval, Fox began an intense spiritual search that led him to consult many of the great preachers of his age and to become so thoroughly familiar with the Old and New Testaments that he knew nearly the whole of them by heart. What he discovered during this search was a Christianity splintered into warring factions, most grasping for State power, while its individual parishes served largely to guarantee a "living" for the sons of aristocrats in the form of a State "tithe" tax. The majority of ministers and priests had little understanding or experience of the faith they were supposedly preaching and they often crassly distorted or baldly misinterpreted Scripture for their own dubious ends.

George Fox's spiritual search led to a series of openings or revelations from God, revelations that emphasized how corrupt, misguided, and shallow the Christianity of his time had become. The first opening he received concerned "how it was said that all Christians are believers," both Catholic and Protestant, but "if all were believers, then they were all born of God and passed from death to life, and...none were true believers but such; and though others said they were believers, yet they were not" [*The Journal of George Fox,* Nickalls edition, 7]. Fox saw that being educated "at Oxford and Cambridge did not qualify or fit a man to be a minister of Christ" and that Fox, himself, if he was to walk rightly, would have to rely wholly upon the Lord Jesus Christ" [*The Journal,* 8]. "At another time," Fox tells us in his *Journal,* "it was opened to me that God, who made the world, did not dwell in temples made with hands..., but that his people were his temple, and he dwelt in them" [8]. The more he studied his Bible, the more he saw that there "was an anointing within man to teach him, and that the Lord would teach his people himself," the very definition of the New Covenant presented in Jeremiah 31:31f. By 1647, Fox had left the priests and preachers of his day, " all those called the most experienced people," for he "saw there was none among them all that could speak to my condition" [*The Journal* 11]. It was then, he tells us:

> When all my hopes in them and in all men were gone, so that I had nothing outwardly to help me, nor could tell what to do, then, Oh then, I heard a voice which said, 'There is one, even Christ Jesus, that can speak to thy condition,' and when I heard it my heart did leap for joy. Then the Lord did let me see why there was none upon the earth that could speak to my condition, namely, that I might give him all the

glory; for all are concluded under sin, and shut up in unbelief as I had been, that Jesus Christ might have the preeminence, who enlightens, and gives grace, and faith, and power.

These early revelations culminated in 1648 with Fox's commission to "proclaim the day of the Lord." "Now," he tells us:

I was sent to turn people from darkness to the light that they might receive Christ Jesus for to as many as should receive him in his light, I saw that he would give power to become sons of God, which I had obtained by receiving Christ. And I was to direct people to the Spirit that gave forth the Scriptures, by which they might be led into all Truth, and so up to Christ and God, as they had been who gave them forth.

In this passage, Fox emphasizes the reason why so many of the "Bible-believing" Christians of his day failed to understand the Scriptures rightly, pursuing State power and violently persecuting one another. They had the Scriptures, but without having the same divine Spirit by which they were written, they could not correctly understand the Book.

So began one of the great ministries in the history of Christianity, one in which Fox declared the good news, that Christ has come to teach and lead His people Himself. Fox traveled throughout England and Wales, on the European continent, in Ireland, and from Georgia to Massachusetts, these latter travels only fifty years after the founding of the Jamestown Colony in Virginia. George Fox, though a man of great physical strength, suffered greatly over the forty years of his ministry. As he traveled and declared the gospel in the early years of Puritan military rule in England (1640s to 1660), his life was repeatedly threatened and he was often severely beaten. With the re-establishment of monarchial government in England in 1660, treatment of Fox and the Quakers hardly improved. Thousands were imprisoned. Others were repeatedly fined for attending meetings for worship and ministering in them, the use of fines being designed to destroy Quakers economically. Imprisoned eight times for preaching and meeting for worship outside the State Church, he (and his fellow Quaker ministers—men and women alike) worked repeatedly for freedom of conscience to worship God, an effort that led to the founding of the Pennsylvania in 1681 by Quaker William Penn, with its guarantee of religious and political freedoms after which the U.S. Bill of Rights was to be modeled in the 18th century.

George Fox died in 1691, finally worn out by the rigors of his ministry, its long imprisonments, beatings, and extraordinary travels. Active until the last, we are told that in worship "he declared a long time very preciously and very audibly and went to prayer." However, after worship, he complained of cold, went to bed, and soon after expired. "According to the witnesses" at his passing," his going was contented and appropriate to his life. They heard him declare, "I am clear, I am fully clear." The great work of the Lord in his life was finished and he passed in peace.

For further study of George Fox and the faith he declared, readers have *The Journal of George Fox*, the John L. Nickalls edition being the finest short version. It is best approached with Joseph Pickvance's *A Reader's Companion to George Fox's Journal* published by the Quaker Home Service in London, 1999. Pickvance's introduction is an excellent help for the reader unfamiliar with the history of 17th century England, 17th century English, and the relevance of George Fox's ministry to our world today. Those who desire to pursue the subject in greater depth will find that an eight volume *Works of George Fox* is available from the publisher of *Quaker-Psalms* as is *None Were So Clear: Prophetic Quaker Faith and the Ministry of Lewis Benson* on the life and scholarship of one of the foremost Fox scholars of the 20th century.

QUAKERPSALMS
from the Journal
of George Fox

QuakerPsalm 1

I Felt the Lord's Power Spread Over All the World in Praise

Praise, honor, and glory to the Lord of heaven
and earth! Lord of peace, Lord of joy!
Your countenance makes my heart glad.
Lord of glory, Lord of mercy, Lord of strength,
Lord of life and of power over death
and Lord of lords and King of kings!

In the world, there are many lords,
but to us there is but one God the Father
and our Lord Jesus Christ, of whom
are all things, to whom be all glory.
In the world are many lords, many gods,
and the earth makes lords, coveting after
riches, oppressing the creatures.[†]

The covetous mind getting to itself,
lords it above others. Lordly pride
is head, until subdued by God's power,
for everyone in that state strives
to be above another. Few strive
to be the lowest.

Oh! That everyone would strive to put down
in themselves mastery and honor, that
the Lord of heaven and earth might be exalted.
Praise, honor, and glory be to the Lord,
Lord of peace, Lord of joy, Lord of strength,
your countenance makes my heart glad!

VII.16

[†]Creatures = Anything created; a created being, animate
or inanimate; a living creature, including a human being
(*OED*).

3

It Is I, Lord, Who Have Done These Things

I saw it was fallen men and women
who get up into Scriptures and find fault,
who cry out against Cain,[†] Esau,[†] and Judas,[†]
and other wicked men of former times,
but do not see the nature of Cain, of
Esau, of Judas in themselves. These say
it is they, they, they, that were bad people.

But when we come, by the Light and Spirit
of Truth, to see into ourselves, then we
come to say "I, I, I, I myself have
been Ishmael,[†] Esau! I have closed my eyes,
stopped my ears, hardened my heart! I was
dull of hearing. I hated the Light. I rebelled
against it. I quenched the Spirit

and vexed and grieved it. I walked spitefully
against the grace of God, turned it
into wantonness. I resisted the Holy Spirit.
I got the form of Godliness, but turned
against the power. I, the ravening wolf,
the well without water, tree without fruit.
It is I, Lord, who have done these things."

I.87

[†]Each person mentioned is an example of a particular inward state. "Cain" killed his brother, Abel, out of envy over Abel's acceptance by God. Thus, Cain is an example of those who hate and persecute the truly faithful. "Judas" was the betrayer of Jesus Christ. "Esau" was the one who sold his spiritual birthright for a single meal, an example of those who toss away their life with God for the cheapest of pleasures. "Ishmael" was the wild ass of a man.

QuakerPsalm 3
There Is One, Even Christ Jesus

When all my hopes in all men were gone,
so that I had nothing outwardly to help me,
nor could tell what to do, then, oh then,
I heard a voice which said, "There is one, even
Christ Jesus, that can speak to your condition,"
and when I heard it my heart did leap for joy.

Then the Lord did let me see why there was
none upon the earth that could speak to my
condition, namely, that I might give Him
the glory, for all are concluded under sin,
and shut up in unbelief as I had been,
that Jesus Christ might have pre-eminence,
who enlightens, gives grace, faith, and power.
And this I knew experimentally.

My desires after the Lord grew stronger
and zeal in the pure knowledge of God
and of Christ alone, without the help of any man,
book or writing. Though I read the scriptures
that spoke of Christ and of God, yet I knew
Him not but by revelation, as He
who has the key did open, and the Father
of Life drew me to His Son by His Spirit.
Now the Lord gently leads me along,

and lets me see His love, which is
endless and eternal and surpasses
all the knowledge that we have in the
natural state, or can get by history
or books. That love lets me see myself
as I was without Him. He it is who
opened me when I was shut up and had

not hope nor faith. Christ it is who
enlightens me, who gives me His Light

to believe in, and gives me hope, which is
Himself, reveals Himself in me and gives
me His Spirit and His grace, which I find
sufficient in the deeps and weaknesses.
In the deepest miseries and sorrows
and temptations that many times beset me,

the Lord in His mercy does keep me.
The Lord in His mercy does keep me.

I.74

QuakerPsalm 4
I Saw into That
Which Was without End

I saw into that which was without end,
things that cannot be uttered, and of the
greatness and infiniteness of God's love,
which cannot be expressed by words.
I had been brought through the very ocean
of darkness and death, and through and over
Satan's power by Christ's glorious power.
Even through that darkness was I brought
which covered the whole world, which chained
down all and shut up all in the death.
God's same eternal power, which brought me
through these things, afterwards shook the nation,
priests, and people. Then I could say, I had been
in spiritual Babylon, Sodom, Egypt, and the grave,
but by God's eternal power, I was brought out
of them into Christ's power. I saw
the harvest white and God's seed lying thick
in the ground, as ever did wheat, and none
to gather: and for this I mourned with tears.

1:80-81

QuakerPsalm 5
I Saw God's Great Love

I saw God's great love and was filled
with admiration at its infiniteness.
I saw what was cast out from God and what
entered into His kingdom, how by Jesus—
the door's opener by His heavenly key—
entrance was given. I saw death, how it
passed upon all and oppressed God's Seed
in man and in me—and how in the Seed
I came forth and what the promise was to.

Yet there seemed to be two pleadings in me
and questionings arose in my mind
about gifts and prophecies, and I was tempted
again to despair, as if I had sinned
against the Holy Spirit.

I was in great perplexity and trouble
for many days—yet I gave myself up
to the Lord still. One day when I walked
solitarily abroad and was come home,
I was taken up in God's love so that
I could not but admire its greatness
and, while I was in that condition, it
was opened† to me by the eternal
Light and Power, and I clearly saw all
was done and to be done in and by Christ:
how He conquers and destroys this tempter,
the devil, and all his works, and is atop him.

When at any time my condition was veiled,
my secret belief stayed firm and hope
underneath held me, as an anchor
in the sea's bottom, and anchored my

8

immortal soul to its bishop, causing it
to swim above the sea, the world,
where all the raging waves, foul weather,
tempests and temptations are.

I:76

---

†*it was opened* = it was revealed

QuakerPsalm 6

Do You Not See
the Blood of Christ

I saw, through the invisible Spirit's
immediate opening,[†] the blood of Christ.
And I cried out among them and said:

"Do you not see the blood of Christ?
See it in your hearts, to sprinkle your hearts
and consciences from dead works to serve
       the living God?"

For I saw it, the blood of the New Covenant,
how it came into the heart, and this startled
those who would have the blood only without them,

and who would not have it within.

I:82

[†]*opening* = revelation

QuakerPsalm 7
Now the Lord Has Opened to Me

Now the Lord has opened to me
by His invisible power
how everyone is enlightened
by Christ's divine Light.

I see it shine through all
and they that believe in it
come out of condemnation
and into the Light of Life

and become children of God,
but they that hate it,
and do not believe in it,
are condemned by it,

though they make a profession[†] of Christ.
I see in that Light and Spirit
which was before Scripture was given forth,
and which led the holy men of God to give them forth:

that all must come to that Spirit,
if they will know God or Christ,
or the Scriptures aright.
All must come to the Spirit

if they will know!

I:89

[†]*profession* = a claim to believe, a claim to be faithful; a formal confession of one's faith. Fox is often critical of those who make a profession, but know neither the power or presence of God in their lives, because their profession is false and hypocritical.

QuakerPsalm 8
Now Am I Come up in Spirit

Now am I come up in Spirit
through the flaming sword
into God's paradise.

All things are new.
All creation gives another fragrance
than before—beyond words.

Now I know nothing but pureness,
innocency, and righteousness,
being renewed up in God's image

by Christ Jesus, so that I can say
I've come up to Adam's state
before he fell.

Yes and I am taken up in Spirit
to see a more steadfast state
than Adam's in innocency:

even into a state in Christ Jesus,
that never should fall.
And the Lord shows me

that such as are faithful to Him,
in Christ's power and Light, should
come up into Adam's state before he fell,

in which the admirable works of creation
and the virtues thereof
may be known through

the openings of that divine word
of wisdom and power
by which they were made.

I:84-85

QuakerPsalm 9

I Found There Were
Two Thirsts in Me

I found there were two thirsts in me,
the one after the creatures,
to have gotten help there,
the other after the Lord the Creator
and His Son Jesus Christ.

And I saw all the world could do me no good.
If I had a king's diet, palace and attendance,
all would have been as nothing,
for nothing gave me comfort
but the Lord in His power.

I saw the priests and people were at ease
in that condition which was my misery
and they love that which I would be rid of.
Yet, the Lord did stay my desires
on Himself from whom my help came,
and my care was cast upon Him alone.

Therefore, all wait patiently upon the Lord,
whatsoever condition you are in.
Wait in the grace and Truth that come by Jesus,
for if you do so, there is a promise to you,
and the Lord God will fulfill it.

Blessed are they indeed that do hunger
and thirst for righteousness.
They shall be satisfied with it.
I have found it so.
O let the spiritual house of Israel say,
"His mercy endures forever."

It is the great love of God to make
a wilderness of that which is pleasant
to the outward eye and fleshly mind,
and to make a barren wilderness
a fruitful field.

This is God's great work,
but while people's minds run in the earthly—
after the creatures and changeable things,
and changeable ways and religions,
uncertain teachers—

their minds are in bondage.
They are brittle and changeable,
tossed up and down with windy doctrines
and thoughts, notions, and things,
their minds being from

the unchangeable Truth in the inward parts,
the Light of Jesus Christ,
who is the way to the faith,
who in my troubles did preserve me
by His Spirit and Power.

I:75

QuakerPsalm 10
There Is a Living God

One morning as I sat,
a great cloud came over me—
but I sat still.

"All things come by nature,"
it was said and the elements
and the stars came over me,
so I was quite clouded.

Yet, people perceived nothing
inasmuch as I sat still
and silent under it

and let it alone.
Then a living hope arose in me
and a true voice said: "There is
a living God who made all things."

Cloud and temptation vanished.
Life arose over all and my heart
danced with gladness
And I praised my living God!

I:83

The Earth in People's Hearts

I saw a great crack go through the earth
and great smoke go up as the crack opened,
and, after the crack, great shaking.

This is the earth in people's hearts
which is shaken before the Seed
of God rises out of it.

The mountains and the rubbish burn—
the heart's high, rough rubbish—
and crooked ways are plained.

To speak of these things seems strange
to the rough, crooked, and mountainous,
but the Lord says, "O Earth, hear

the word of the Lord!"
In the low region,
in the airy life,

all news is uncertain.
There's nothing
stable. But

in the higher region, Christ's kingdom,
all things are stable and sure,
and the news always good and certain,

for Christ, who has all power in heaven
and earth, rules the kingdoms of men.
His power is certain and does not change.

He shakes and shatters old heavens and earth,
levels the mountains and hills, and, though the
faithless neither see it nor know Him—

the faithful do. Yes, the faithful do.

I:81 & I:77

16

QuakerPsalm 12

Don't Let Your Mind
Go Forth from God

—From Darby Gaol, 1650

1 - The Lord Shows Our Thoughts

The Lord shows us our thoughts
and discovers all our secret workings.
He brings us to see our evil thoughts,
our running mind and vain imagination.

We may strive to keep them down, but
can't overcome them nor keep to the Lord.

So submit to the Lord in this condition,
He who discovers them—the root of lusts
and vain imaginations, how they are begotten,
how bred and brought forth—He will destroy them.

We may strive to keep them down, but
can't overcome them nor keep to the Lord.

So mind the faith of Christ—the anointing
that is in you—to be taught by it.
It will discover all workings in you
and, as Christ teaches you, so obey

and forsake: else you will not grow up
in faith, nor in Christ's Life where God

is received. Love begets love, its own
nature and image, and when mercy and Truth
do meet, what joy there is! So mind the faith
of Christ, the anointing that is in you.

2 - Evil's But One in All

Some men and women have the nature
of swine and wallow in mire;

and some the nature of dogs, to bite
both the sheep and each other;

and some have the lion's nature, some
the wolf's, to tear, devour, and destroy;

and some the serpent's nature,
to sting, envenom, and poison;

and some the horse's, to prance
and vapor, strong in evil,

minding nothing but earthly things,
feeding without the fear of God.

Evil is but one in all, but works
in many ways: and whatsoever we are

addicted to, the Evil One will fit us
with it, and please our appetites

to keep our mind from our Creator.
When it gets into flesh and death,

then the Accuser gets within,
then the Life suffers under sin,

and we know straightness and failings.
Then the good is shut up, then

self-righteousness climbs atop
and we labor in the outward law.

Then we may strive to keep it down,
but cannot overcome nor keep to the Lord.

3 - Don't Let Your Mind Go Forth

Oh, don't let your mind go forth from God!
If it does, it will be stained, venomed,
and corrupted! If it does go forth,
it is hard to bring it in again—

but as the Lord who is invisible
opens you by His invisible power
and Spirit, the invisible, immortal
things are brought to light you.

Oh, you that know the Light, walk in it,
for there are children of darkness
that will talk of the Light and Truth,
but not walk in it.

The earthly lusts
and carnal mind
choke the Seed of faith
and bring oppression in, and death.

Oh, mind the pure Spirit of God
which will teach you to use the creatures
in their rightful place, to live
and walk in joy and peace and Life.

There is peace in resting in the Lord,
there is peace. There is peace. Peace.

I:106-108

19

God's People Should Be Like unto Him

God is righteous,
and He would have His people to do righteously.

God is holy,
and He would have His people holy.

God is just,
and would have His people to do justly to all.

God is Light,
and His children must walk in the Light.

God is an eternal, infinite Spirit,
and His children must walk in the Spirit.

God is merciful,
and He would have His people to be merciful.

God's sun shines upon the good and the bad,
and he causes the rain to fall upon

the evil and the good—
and so should His people do good to all.

God is love
and they that dwell in love, dwell in God.

Love works no ill to his neighbor.

II:322

QuakerPsalm 14
God Would Have All to Be Saved

God, who is merciful,
would have all to be saved
and come to Truth's knowledge.
All who come to that knowledge

must know it in their inward parts.
All that know and find the grace
and Truth that comes by Jesus
know and find them in their hearts.

Such find the heart's hidden
man, the pearl, the leaven,
the lost piece of silver,
and God's kingdom within.

II:319

Sound, Sound Abroad, You Faithful Servants

—To Friends in the Ministry, 1669

Sound, sound abroad, you faithful servants
of the Lord, witnesses in His name, prophets
of the Highest, angels of the Lord!

Sound you all abroad in the world
to awaken and raise the dead out of
the grave to hear the voice that is living—

for the dead have long heard the dead,
the blind long wandered among the blind,
and the deaf among the deaf.

Therefore, sound, sound, you servants, prophets,
angels, you trumpets of the Lord, that
you may awaken the dead, them that are

asleep in their graves of sin, death,
and hell, sea and earth,
who lie in the tombs.

Sound, sound abroad, you trumpets, raise
up the dead, that the dead may hear
the voice of God's Son, the second

Adam's voice, the voice of the Light,
the Life, the power, the Truth,
the righteous, the just. Sound!

Sound the pleasant melodious
sound. Sound, sound you the trumpets,
the melodious sound abroad,

that all the deaf ears may be opened
to hear the trumpet's pleasant sound
to judgment and Life, condemnation

and Light. Sound, sound your trumpets
all abroad, you angels of the Lord,
sons and daughters, prophets of the Highest,

that all that are dead and asleep
in the graves, who have long dreamed
and slumbered, who've long heard the beast's

voice, may wake and hear the Lamb's voice,
the Bridegroom's, the bride's, the great Prophet's,
the great King's, the great Shepherd's voice.

Sound, sound it all abroad, you trumpets,
among Adam's dead, for Christ is
come, the second Adam, that they

might have Life, yes, have it abundantly.
Awaken the dead, awaken
the slumberers, the dreamers,

awaken them out of their graves,
tombs, sepulchres, seas! Sound, sound
abroad, you trumpets, that they may

all hear and they that hear may live
and come to the Life, God's Son. He's
risen from the dead. The grave could not

hold him, nor could all the watchers
of the earth with all their guards!
Sound, sound, you trumpets of the Lord—

to all the seekers of the living
among the dead in the graves that
the watchers keep—that He's risen,

He's not in the grave, He's risen.
There's that under the grave of the
watchers of the outward grave,

which must be awakened and come
to hear His voice that they might live.
Therefore, sound abroad, you trumpets

of the Lord, that the grave might give
up her dead, that hell and the sea
might give up their dead and all might

come forth to judgment according to their works.

II:88-89

QuakerPsalm 16
Bring All into God's Worship

—To those who minister

Bring all into God's worship.
Plow up the fallow ground.
Thresh and get out the corn, that the seed,
the wheat, may be gathered into the barn;
that all people may come to the beginning,
to Christ, who was before the world was made.

He that treads it out is without transgression,
fathoms transgression, puts a difference
between the precious and the vile,
can pick out the wheat from the tares,
and gather into the garner.

None are plowed up but those
who come to God's principle within,
God's principle which they have transgressed.
Then they do service to God.
Then is the planting, watering,
and increase from God.

I:288

Christ Is Both Head
and Husband of His Church

Feel Christ's presence among you,
to exercise His prophetical office
to opening His Light, Grave, Truth,
Power, and Spirit—Christ, the
second Adam, who is both Head
and Husband of His church, Redeemer,
Purchaser, Savior, Sanctifier,
and Reconciler of His sons
and daughters to God.

As Christ is a shepherd, feel, see,
and hear Him exercising that office,
who has laid down His life for His sheep,
feeds them in His living pastures,
and makes them drink of His eternal springs.

Let Him rule and govern in your hearts,
as He is King, that all may live
under His heavenly and spiritual
government, as true subjects
of His righteous, peaceable kingdom—
His kingdom which stands in joy
in the Holy Ghost over Satan
and his power, the unclean, the
unholy ghost, and all unrighteousness.

All you subjects of Christ's kingdom
of peace, Christ is the treasure,
if you want wisdom, knowledge, Life
or salvation. Feel Him, the treasure
among you. Everyone, as you
have received Christ, walk in Him

in whom you have peace, who bruises
the serpent's head, the author of
all strife, distraction, and confusion:
yes, you have peace with God and one
another, though the trouble be
from the world and the world's spirit.

II:240

QuakerPsalm 18

Keep over the Spirit of Separation and Division

Keep over the spirit
of separation and division.
Keep in the peaceable Truth
and in the Seed of life
which will wear it all out.
The Lamb will have the victory
over all strife's spirits,
as it has had since the
beginning. They will wither
as others have done, but
all that keep in the Seed,
which is always green,
shall never wither.

If any have backslidden,
thrown off the cross,
grown loose and full,
gone into strife and contention
with their earthly spirits,
and plead *liberty*: this spirit
takes with loose earthly spirits
and cries "imposition!"
to such as admonish them
to come to God's Life, Light,
Spirit, and Power, that
they may be made alive
and live again with the living.

These dead would have Truth's name,
but not Truth's nature.
These dead deceive, but are judged
by that which undeceives and saves.

II:191

Be Not Amazed at the Weather

Be not amazed at the weather,
for always
the just suffered by the unjust,

But the just have dominion.
All along,
faith subdued the mountains and quenched

the rage of the wicked with their
fiery darts.
Though the waves and storms be high,

yet your faith will keep you to swim
above them.
They're but for a time; Truth is without time.

Keep on the holy mountain where
nothing shall hurt,
you who are led to it by the Light.

Do not think anything will out-
last the Truth,
which stands sure and is over that

which is out of the Truth:
because the good
will overcome the evil,

the Light darkness, the Life death,
virtue vice,
and righteousness unrighteousness.

The false prophet cannot over-
come the true,
but the true prophet, Christ,

will overcome all the false.
So be faithful
and live in that which does not think

the time long.

II:103-104

QUAKERPSALMS
from the Epistles
of George Fox

QuakerPsalm 20
No One Is Justified

No one is justified
who breaks Christ's commands,
lives in wickedness,
professes only Christ's words
and the prophets'
and the apostles' words
while living out of their lives.

Therefore, mind God's power.
No. No one is justified
who lives in the first birth,
false faith and false hope,
which does not purify as God is pure;
who doesn't believe in Christ's Light;
who acts contrary
to the Spirit which convinces.

Epistle 6

QuakerPsalm 21
The Lamb Shall Have the Victory

That which is set up by the sword
is held up by the sword;
and that set up by spiritual weapons
is held up by spiritual weapons.

The peacemaker has the kingdom
and is in it, has dominion
over the peacebreaker
to calm him in God's power.

Let the waves break over your heads.
A new and living way is rising,
which makes the nations like waters.
Hurt not the vines, nor the oil,

nor such as know that "the earth
is the Lord's and the fullness thereof."
The days of virtue, love, and peace
are come and coming. The Lamb had

and has the kings of the earth to war
withal—the Lamb who will overcome
with the sword of the Spirit, the word
of His mouth, and shall have the victory.

Epistle 9

QuakerPsalm 22
Stand Still and See

—In times of temptation

The tempter will come
in what you're addicted[†] to,
and when he troubles you,
he gets advantage over you.

Stand still in what is pure
after you see yourselves,
for then mercy comes in.

After you see your thoughts
and temptations,
do not think, but submit,
for then the power comes.

Stand still in that which shows
and discovers, for then
strength instantly comes.

Sink down in what is pure
and all will be hushed
and fly away.
Stand still in Christ and see.

Whatever you see
yourselves addicted to,
you think you will

never overcome,
and earthly reason will
tell you what you shall lose.
Don't listen to it,

but stand in Christ's Light
that shows what is evil
and then the Lord's strength comes—

help contrary to expectation.
Then you grow up in peace;
no trouble shall move you.
David fretted himself

when he looked out,
but when he was still,
no trouble could move him.

Come, stay your minds upon
the Spirit beyond the letter,
for here you learn to read
the scriptures rightly.

If you do anything
in your own wills,
then you tempt God.

So stand still in His power.
Stand still.
Stand
still.

Epistle 10

---

†*addicted* = Moderns think of this word chiefly in refer-
ence to drug use, but 17ᵗʰ century usage meant giving
oneself frequently or persistently to an indulgence, prac-
tice, etc., in Fox's reference: a wrong indulgence or
practice. It suggests a pathological weakness.

QuakerPsalm 23
Wait to Feed on
the Immortal Food

Dear hearts, brethren, and babes in Christ:
wait to feed on the immortal food
and walk in the Truth
and God Almighty be among you.
In it, you will see Him.

Stand all naked and uncovered before Him.
Take heed of your will, for that
(like Herod) slays the just,
shipwrecks the faith,
and runs you into the flesh.

Return. Stay yourselves upon the Lord
in every particular,
to have your minds guided by His Spirit.
Growing up in that which is precious
and immortal, there is no feigned love.

So the eternal God keep you
in His eternal love, pure
unto Himself, naked, and knit
your hearts together. God Almighty
bless you, and water you with the showers

of His mercy, and the heavenly dew.

Epistle 11

Prize Your Time

Prize your time
and the Lord's love for you
above all things.

Mind the Light in you which shows you evil,
which checks you,
when you speak an evil word, and tells you
you should not
be proud, nor wanton, nor fashion yourselves
like the world,
for the world's fashion passes away.

Mind the Light. It will keep your mind humble,
heart lowly,
and turn the mind within to wait upon
the Lord,
to be guided by Him. Mind the Light.
It will bring you
to lay aside all evil, to wait on Christ

for teaching till an entrance be made
to your hearts
and refreshment come from His presence there.
Mind the Light
and it will not allow you to conform
to the world's
evil customs, fashions, delight, vanities.

It will lead to pureness, rightness, even
up to the Lord.
Dear hearts, listen to it, be guided by it,
for if you love
the Light, you love Christ, but if you hate it,

you hate Christ.
The Lord open your understandings to know Him.

Mind the Lord's
love for you and mind the Light
above all things.

Epistle 17

QuakerPsalm 25
For Suffering Friends

The Lord's everlasting arm hold you up,
break all your bonds asunder,
and set you on your feet upon the rock

where you may know His presence,
and His everlasting supreme power.
And so the God of Life be with you!

Now pray for your enemies,
for the Lord to open them and their hearts,
to see themselves and you.

Epistle 30

QuakerPsalm 26
Stand up You Prophets
of the Lord

Stand up, you prophets of the Lord,
for the Truth upon the earth.
Quench not your prophecy,
neither heed them that despise it,
but stand in that which brings
you through to the end.

Heed not the world's eyes, you prophets
of the Lord, but answer that in them all,
which they have closed their eye to,
that you may tell of things to come.

Keep to your habitations,
you sons of God, that you may
reign over all the contrary.
You daughters, to whom it
is given to prophesy,
keep within your own measure.

See over that which is without,
answering that of God in all.
Do not despise prophecy.
Keep down the nature that would,
the same nature that acts
contrary to God in all people.

Neither be lifted up by your
openings and prophecies,
lest you depart from that
which is opened and so come
to be judged by the Son of God,
and bidden to depart as workers of iniquity.

Quench not the Spirit, by which you
may prove all things, and to that
which is good, hold fast. If you
quench the Spirit, then Light
is mistaken for darkness, and darkness
for Light. Evil is confused with good

and good with evil. If you quench
the Spirit, you cannot try all things
or hold fast to that which is good.
You cannot see the good, for the Spirit
proves all things and sorts the precious
from the vile, the profane from the holy,

the clean from the unclean. With the Spirit,
you will see the good, to take the good,
and shun the evil. Stand up, you prophets
of the Lord, for the Truth upon the earth.
Quench not the Spirit, but stand in that
which brings you through to the end.

Epistle 35

Dwell in That Which Is Pure

Dwell in that which is pure and wait
for God's power to preserve you in it.
Know God's Seed in one another that your
knowledge after the flesh may die.
Know God's power in one another.
Let your faith stand in that which throws
out the earthly nature and man's loftiness,
which overturns worldly wisdom and the
carnal knowledge[†] which is brutish, devilish.

Dwell in that which is pure that you
may be able to discern, and savour,[†]
and comprehend that which is not pure.
Wait in that which is pure, to have
your minds guided thereby,
which will let you see God,
and show you your evil thoughts
and judge them. That which is pure is
a cross to your evil desires and wills.

Dwell in that which is pure,   .
which will guide you to God—
but if you lust, the pure is veiled,
the light mind speaks at random
with a drunken spirit,
and not from the Lord's mouth.
There lodges the dreamer,[†] the lying
Spirit, the false prophet, that which is
like Truth, but is not Truth.

Dwell in the Truth and discover this—
dwell in that which is pure.

Epistle 50

43

†*Carnal knowledge* = not spiritual, unregenerated, unsanctified, merely worldly, animal knowledge (OED).
†*Savour* = to perceive, apprehend; to discover traces of (OED)
†*Dreamer* = one who indulges in fancies or daydreams, who forms imaginary visions of unrealities; who acts drowsily or indolently, who procrastinates.

QuakerPsalm 28
Do Not Make Flesh Your Arm

Do not make flesh your arm
by carnal reasonings,
consultations,
and disputings
in that part which is above
the innocent life:

for innocence needs none
to plead its cause,
but God its Father,
who will give you
sufficient strength
and wisdom at the same hour.

The other fails before
God's enemies.

Epistle 59

45

QuakerPsalm 29
Know the Life

Know God's life and power
in yourselves and one another,
and to that power be obedient
to thresh down all deceit
within and without you in wisdom.

Dwell in that which comprehends
the world. Know the rest for God's people,
which those that believe have entered.
Know the life that stands in God
and all know the power of God,

for that power shall never be
shaken nor change, but will shake down
all that must be shaken and will change.
The Lord God Almighty preserve you,
who gives you to see where

there is no changing nor shadow.

Epistle 68

Now the Beast Opens His Mouth

— A warning against false religious teachers,
preachers, and priests who persecute

Wait upon God to learn of
and to be taught by Him, for
now the Beast opens his mouth,
speaking great swelling words.
Now the cage of unclean birds
and the unclean spirits are seen,
which are gone forth into the earth.
Now are the locusts seen
and the caterpillars known.
Now the seven thunders utter
their voices. Now the hailstones
fall and the vials of God's wrath
pour out upon the Beast
and false prophet. Now
the whited walls are seen, the
painted sepulchres who garnish
the sepulchres of the righteous
and build tombs to the prophets,
full of dead men's bones. Now
are the inwardly ravening wolves
seen, which have gotten sheep's
clothing, and now are the false
prophets seen who make merchandise
of the people, who would murder,
and do murder in their hearts.
Now the unsavoury things
are smelled, tasted, and seen
among many who claim religion,
but are more like swine or dogs

that rend, bite, or devour
one another, than like
the children of light—
the children of light
whom they mock and stone,
the children of light
many of whom they have
almost murdered.
Now are such deceivers seen
and known, who speak a
divination of their own brain
and use their tongues and say
the Lord sent them,
when He never has.

VII:98-99   *Epistle 91*

QuakerPsalm 31
Have Hold of the
Truth in Yourselves

Don't be carried away by good words and fair speeches,
nor the affectionate part which is taken with them,[†]

> but have hold of the Truth in yourselves,
> the Most High's Life and Light and Power
> by which you may be stayed upon Christ
> your bread—Christ your bread, the staff
> of your heavenly and eternal life.

You who have denied the world's songs and singing:

> sing in the Spirit, and with grace,
> making melody in your hearts to the Lord.

You who have denied the world's prayings:

> pray always in the Spirit and watch for it.

You who have denied the world's giving thanks,

> its saying of grace and living out of it:
> give thanks in everything to the Lord through
> Jesus Christ.

You that have denied the world's praising God

> with its lips, while its heart is far off,
> always praise the Lord night and day.

You that have denied the world's fastings,

> its hanging down its head like a bulrush
> for a day, while it smites with fists of wickedness:

> keep the Lord's fast that breaks iniquity's bonds
> and lets the world go free,

that your health may grow
  and your Light shine like the morning.

Epistle 167

†Fox is no enemy of the affections or of good words. Rather, he warns us not to be lured away from true worship and right action by glib rhetoric and cunningly tailored arguments designed to appeal to our affections and seduce us from living in Truth.

QuakerPsalm 32
Keep in the Power
and Seed of God

Keep in the power and Seed of God
      in which you will live in the Substance.

Take heed of running on in a form,
      lest you lose the power.

Take heed at any disputes:
      many may be lifted up
      in victory and conquest, have joy
      in the prophesies and openings,

      and after fall.

If babblers come and janglers say
      they "have a bad Meeting,"
      the murmuring nature gets up,
      out of patience
      and the Seed.

The Seed bears all things,
      suffers all things, keeps down
      that which causes lifting up,
      murmuring, and disputing.

The Seed and prophecy[†] keep down and end
      all that is contrary
      and would live so.

The Peace,
the Cornerstone,
the Seed
      is that which keeps down
      that which changes.

Epistle 173

†*Prophecy* = in the Old Testament sense, the prophet, inspired by God, brings words from the Lord to call the people to the right way of living, to justice and to mercy. These roles far transcend the common misunderstanding that prophets merely predict the future. They foretell on the bases of what God reveals to them and of the natural outcome of wrongdoing.

QuakerPsalm 33

All Friends, You Must Come[†]

All Friends, you must come into a temperance
        above the world.

Friends, you must come into a patience, a moderation
        above the world.

You must all come into a wisdom, a knowledge,
an understanding,
        above the world.

Come all into a sobriety, and gravity, a seasoned state
        above the world.

All Friends, you must.

[†]Based on George Fox's Epistle 179. This epistle was inad-
vertently printed without heading in the 1698 and 1831 edi-
tions of Fox's *Works*. T. Canby Jones notes that the style
and content of the latter part of Epistle 178 are so different that
the latter part must be Epistle 179. See *"The Power of the
Lord is Over All": The Pastoral Letters of George Fox*,
edited by T. Canby Jones. (Richmond, IN: Friends United
Press, 1989), p.iv.

Sing and Rejoice,
Children of the Day

—For those in Christ who suffer persecution

Sing and rejoice
you children of the Day and of the Light!

Sing and rejoice!
Christ is at work in this tangible darkness.

Truth flourishes like the rose and lilies
grow among the thorns upon the hilltops.

The lambs skip and play upon them. The lambs
do skip and play.

Never heed the rains, the floods, the storms,
the torrents, tempests,

for Christ reigns over all. Be of good faith,
be of good faith,

valiant for the Truth, for the Truth can live
in jails.

Never fear the loss of fleece, for it will
grow again.

Follow the Lamb, even under the Beast's
horns and heels,

For the Lamb shall have the victory
over all.

Live in Christ, your way that never fell
and you will see

Over all the ways of Adam's and Eve's
daughters and sons

in the Fall. So stand and dwell in Christ,
your Life and peace,

the Life that was with the Father before
the world began,

the Life that was with the Father before
the world began,

the Life that was with the Father before
the world began.

Epistle 227

Never Heed

Live in the everlasting Power, Life, and Truth,
for you cannot live without them in winds and storms.

Though the hills and mountains burn,
the trees become fruitless,
the winter devours the former fruits,
and you see that persecution has choked them,
and the heat scorches them—

though the untimely figs fall,
the corn withers on the housetop,
the night comes, and the evil beasts
go out of their dens, Truth lives
and God's power is over them all.

Christ rules and in Him and His house is Life's
                    bread and water,
though caterpillars and locusts agree to
                    eat up all the green.

All who are in the Truth rejoice through Christ
and mind Him who has all seasons in His hand.

Never heed prisons,
for they are but for a time.
Never heed the sea's raging waves
nor be troubled at his tongue that speaks nothing
but tribulation, anguish, and bondage,

nor be troubled at the cords of the ungodly,
for love's cords, God's power, are stronger.
What does He do that sits in heaven,
but laugh them to scorn?
So be valiant for the Truth upon the earth,

for the power is the Lord's, all my dear Friends,
in the everlasting seed that never fell or changes.

Epistle 236

QuakerPsalm 36

Keep to Your Habitation and First Love

All everywhere, keep to your habitation
and your first love. Do not go forth
from your rule of faith and Life within,

where you all have unity and fellowship
and the Lord will be your Comforter and Teacher.

If you do not go forth from the Light, Spirit,
and Truth within, you will feel the Light
to guide and lead, and instruct you.

You may have immortality put
upon you by it, so be not ashamed
of Christ Jesus the Light and Life, and Teacher,
nor of His Spirit to lead you,

for they can find no occasion against you
but that you worship God in Spirit
and obey the command of Christ Jesus.

As the old cry was, "away with such from the earth,
it is not fit for them to live," so it is now.

Yet, blessed are those who keep their habitations
clean, and live in the Lord's power,
which was before the curse.

Epistle 238

This Is Your Day to Stand

This is your day to stand in Him
that stood steadfast,
and reigned over old Adam,
the devil, and all persecutors.

Old Adam did not stand,
but Christ, the second Adam,
the heavenly man, stood
and never fell.

In Him stand,
for now is your time
to stand in the Life over death,
in the Light over darkness,

and the Seed that bruises
the serpent's head, the Seed
in whom you have Life,
dominion, and peace.

The Lord is coming upon the wicked
in His thundering power,
for they are ripe.
They're corrupt with blood,

their flesh rotten:
they've fallen into the pit,
being led by blind guides
into the pit and ditches,

where they rot and stink,
being putrefied with the heat
of their lusts. All my dear
Friends, this is your day to stand.

Epistle 243

QuakerPsalm 38
Dwell in the Lord's Gentle Wisdom

Dwell in the Lord's gentle wisdom,
which is easy to be entreated.
Do not let willfulness,
or hastiness, or impatience,
lay open your nakedness to the world.

Dwell in Christ Jesus' Life, Seed,
and Power, God's wisdom. With it,
you all may be kept clothed in patience,
in God's love, and in the Light, in which
is unity one with another and with God.

Dwell in the peaceable mind and Spirit,
for the patient sufferer wears the crown
and has the victory at last—not the
hasty, aggravating, revengeful, killing
spirit which must be crushed down,

the serpent's head, the cause of enmity
and venom. When the head is crushed
by Christ's Seed, nothing is fed upon
but Life and glory and in that is peace.
Dwell in the Lord's gentle wisdom.

Epistle 245

If a Child Be Fallen down in the Dirt

No man, after he has punished a child,
hates him ever afterwards, but loves him
if he repents and amends—and so does God.

If a child be fallen down in the dirt,
he does not go and tumble him more in the ditch
and there let him lie—but takes him out

washes him. So does our heavenly parent
who leads His children by His hand
and dandles them upon His knee.

So all that are called fathers or mothers
in the Truth, their tenderness should be
the same to all little children

in the Truth, who can hardly go without leading,
Who sometimes may fall into the dirt
and ditch and slip aside, and then

be troubled and cry. To such there should be
tenderness shown, to wash and help them.
Yes, love should be shown. Love should be shown.

Epistle 262a

QuakerPsalm 40
Let Execution Be Speedily Done

That's to be condemned in yourselves
which has led you from Christ.
That is condemned and must be executed,
stoned with the living Stone,
run through with the living Sword,

hammered down to pieces
with the living Hammer,
burned up with the living Fire—
and so made an end of.

That which leads into looseness,
whimsies, imaginations, false visions,
though it be condemned, yet,
if it be not executed,
is in danger to rise again.

And if it rise again,
if it get out of prison
alive and get over you,
it will be your ruler.

Therefore, after judgment is passed,
let execution be speedily done
with the living Hammer, Sword, and Stone,
that the living Fire may burn
and consume it.

Epistle 262b

QuakerPsalm 41
Let All Keep Their Habitation

All dear Friends everywhere,
who have no helper but the Lord
who is your strength and your Life,

let your cries and prayers be to Him
who with His eternal power has kept
your heads above all waves and storms.

Let none go out of their habitation—
whose habitation is in the Lord—
in the stormy time of the night.

Let all keep their habitation
and stand in their lot, the Seed, Christ
Jesus, to the end of the day.

There's the lot of your inheritance.
In this Seed you will see the bright
and morning star appear, which will

expel the night of darkness that has
been in your hearts. By this morning
star, you will come to everlasting day,

this bright morning star in your heart.

Epistle 280

QuakerPsalm 42
The Lord God's Counsel to You All

Live in love, for this is of God
and edifies the body of Christ.

Keep in God's Truth, which the devil
is out of. Walk in the same

peaceable Truth. Do righteously
to all people, walk in righteousness,

and then you will walk in peace
with God and one another. Walk

in holiness, for that becomes
the house of God. In holiness,

you will see our God among you.
Dwell in love one with another,

so that you may keep the unity
in the Spirit, the bond of peace,

because all eyes are upon you
and some watch for evil.

Do answer the good in all,
in your words and lives.

This is the Lord God's counsel
to you all, that you may be

the salt of the earth,
the light of the world,

the city set on a hill
that cannot be hid.

Epistle 290

QuakerPsalm 43
The Truth Is above All

The Truth is above all
and will stand over all them that hate it,
who labor in vain against it
and will bring their old house on their own heads
to their great trouble.

In the winter,
when their house is down,
their religion frozen,
their rivers dried up,
their husks gone and the swine
begin to cry upon the plantations
and the vermin run up and down
against their old rubbish,
and their sparks and candles
are gone out, and hail and storms strike:
then woe to the wicked who have no covering.

In Christ you have peace;
in the world you have trouble.
No peace with God can be enjoyed
but in the covenant of Light.
Without it is trouble; without it is trouble.

Epistle 294

The Danger of Husks the Swineherd Feeds His Swine

At the first convincement,[†]
there's not so much danger
for the Spirit of God
keeps in the fear of the Lord
and under judgment.

Then after getting acquaintance
or knowledge, a familiarity
and a liberty, but
not in the Holy Spirit,
there is great danger.

Your knowledge and familiarity
must be in the invisible
Spirit, for the flesh fades
and withers as grass.
The Lord's Word endures forever.

Right knowledge of one
another is this: to know one
another in the Word
which was in the beginning
before man and woman fell.

We do not live by bread
alone, but by every word
from the mouth of God—
not the husks the swineherd
feeds to his swine.

We do not live by bread
alone, but by every word

from the mouth of God—
the fresh and heavenly
food from above.

Epistle 295

---

†*Convincement* = The original Quaker word for conversion. Convincement refers to far more than mere intellectual persuasion. It means, also, to be convinced or convicted of the wrong that one has done, the sin; to feel the judgment of God within oneself; to feel with one's whole being God's loving redemption; and to begin to know the power of God to overcome the sinful person within us and to enable us to walk in His will.

QuakerPsalm 45
Let All Things Be Done in Love

Let all things be done in love,
and kindness, affableness,
courteousness—what is
decent, comely, of a good
report in God's eyes and all
good people's hearts.

Strive not for mastery,
but let Christ be master.
Dwell in humility
and love that will bear all
things, that is not easily provoked,
that does not envy—for,

if your love is not in this love,
it is not the love of God.

Let all things be done in love,
so that nothing may be seen
of the old heaven, old
malice, old man—his deeds
and image, his old bottle,
his sour grapes. Do not eat them,
for, if you do, they will set
your teeth on edge, one against another.

Mind the royal Seed. Christ
Jesus, that new and living way,
a new man after God and His image
who makes all things new—
the new leaven that leavens up
into God's love, that builds
up the body of Christ.

You are the new bottles,
full of new wine from Christ
the vine—the new wine
which makes all your hearts glad
to God and Christ and one in another.

Epistle 311

QuakerPsalm 46
Christ Is the Treasure

If you want wisdom and knowledge to order you
in God's affairs and service,
Christ is the treasure,
so receive them from His treasury above.

This is the saving wisdom in which you have
your grace and Truth, Light and Life, and the gospel,
the heavenly Spirit—yes, heavenly food
and bread, water of life from above,
the unleavened bread and the Word's
sweet milk, to keep the heavenly man's passover.

These aren't found in any of old Adam's
sons' and daughters' storehouses.
His old, moldy, leavened, sour bread
makes his sons' and daughters' hearts burn
against one another.
They cloth themselves with his old rags—
rags which will not cover their nakedness,
rags they have stitched together,
rags which must be cast off
and trodden under foot by Christ's Spirit
and power, Christ who clothes all His sons
and daughters with His heavenly fine linen,
linen which never waxes old.

Therefore, let all your lamps be trimmed
and candles lighted, that all of you may see
your work and service for God and Christ.

Epistle 365

QuakerPsalm 47
Prize the Lord's Mercies

Prize the Lord's mercies
and live in humility,
in His power that is over all,
in His Spirit and Truth,
in righteousness, in godly life
and conversation, that you may
answer God's witness in all people.

Let not liberty lift you up,
nor sufferings cast you down;
but live in the Seed of Life,
that no one can make higher
or lower. The Seed is the heir
of God's everlasting kingdom.

God Almighty keep you in this Seed,
this Seed in which you have Life,
this Seed your sanctuary
and wisdom, that wisdom may be
justified of all her children.

Epistle 413

Nothing Can Make You Turn from Christ

Brothers and sisters in the Lord Jesus Christ—

who, by His eternal arm and power,
has supported, upheld,
and preserved you steadfast to Himself—

neither reproaches,

nor the spoiling of your goods
to almost outward ruin,

nor long and tedious imprisonments
even to the death of many,

can make you turn from Christ
your Life, Priest, Bishop, and Shepherd.

You are made more than conquerors through Him,

so live and walk in Him
in whom you have Life, salvation, and peace,
who is the same yesterday, today, and forever,
who overcomes and will have the victory,

who overcomes, who will have the victory.

Epistle 414

Epilogue

Now All Creatures Stand in Their Places Keeping Their Unity†

A man is brought up
or led by Christ his leader
into the image of God,
into righteousness and holiness.

Through this, man has a dominion
over all that God made,
subduing the earth,
reigning over it as a king.

He comes to God as he walks
in righteousness, in Truth,
in the Light and the power of God.
All things become new to him in Christ Jesus,
who makes all things new.

Man walks as under a curtain,
and as in a garden;
all things are sweet and pleasant to him,
and every thing gives a sweet smell.

The heavens above are garnished,
like a curtain, with the sun, moon, and stars;
the earth under him is clothed
with grass and trees and herbs;
and man walks as in a garden under curtains.

But as a man has lost
the righteousness and holiness,
and the prince of darkness corrupts him,
this is a sad walking.

Man's sight, his smell, his hearing, his sight
of heavenly things, invisible and immortal things,
and eternal and divine things,
are taken away, are taken away.

This is a mystery and riddle to man.
Therefore, let all people consider
what a doleful, sad condition
they walk in.

Christ leads them to peace and joy and comfort.
He that believes in the Light sees
the joy, the comfort, the paradise,
the garden of God, the garden of pleasure.

He that believes sees how they walk under curtains,
how God has garnished the heavens,
and clothed the earth with grass and trees and herbs
how all the creatures stand in their places,
keeping their unity.

He sees the sun and moon in their courses,
and the stars keeping the law of God's covenant,
and how all the creatures stand in their places,
how all the creatures stand in their places,
keeping their unity.

---

†I thank Godwin Arnold of Reading, England, for calling
this particular psalm to my attention, suggesting it for the
collection. My rendering comes from a text in Hugh McG.
Ross's *A Collected Set of Passages from George Fox's
Writings* printed in mimeograph copy in July, 1978. The
text is a much shortened extract from manuscript 61E Aa,
bound with *The Annual Catalogue of George Fox's Papers*.
The original was dictated in 1669.